STARS OF
THE WORLD CUP

Abbeville Press Publishers

New York • London

A portion of the proceeds from this book are donated
to the **Hugo Bustamante AYSO Playership Fund,** a
national scholarship program to help ensure that
no child misses the chance to play AYSO Soccer.
Donations cover the cost of registration and a uniform
for a child in need.

Pages 2–3: The Spanish national team after winning the 2010 World Cup
final against the Netherlands in Johannesburg, South Africa.

Text by Illugi Jökulsson and Björn Thor Sigbjörnsson

For the original edition
Designer: Árni Torfason

For the English-language edition
Editor: David Fabricant
Copy editor: Ashley Benning
Production manager: Louise Kurtz
Designer: Paul Aljian

Photography credits
Getty Images: front cover, back cover (center, bottom left), pp. 2, 4, 6, 13, 14, 17, 29, 39
(inset), 42, 48, 54, 58, 60, 62
Shutterstock: back cover (top, bottom right), pp. 4, 8, 10, 16, 18, 22, 23, 24, 27, 28, 30, 32, 34,
37, 38, 40, 42, 50, 52, 56
Árni Torfason: pp. 4, 46, 47

First published in the United States of America in 2014 by Abbeville Press, 137 Varick Street,
New York, NY 10013

First published in Iceland in 2013 by Sögur útgáfa, Fákafen 9, 108 Reykjavík, Iceland

ISBN 978-0-7892-1211-5

Library of Congress Cataloging-in-Publication Data available upon request

For bulk and premium sales and for text adoption procedures, write to
Customer Service Manager, Abbeville Press, 137 Varick Street, New York, NY 10013,
or call 1-800-Artbook.

Visit Abbeville Press online at www.abbeville.com.

CONTENTS

Agüero playing for Argentina against Peru in October 2013. The nickname "Kun" on the back of his jersey was given to him when he was a kid, because he looked like the little cartoon dog Kun Kun!

Kun Kun.

AGÜERO
Striker
Argentina
Born 1988
Plays for
Manchester City

AGÜERO
The Argentinean Dynamo

Sergio "Kun" Agüero was born in Quilmes, Argentina, on June 2, 1988. He got his break with Independiente's senior side just after he turned 15, making him the youngest player ever in the Argentinean top league—breaking the legendary Diego Maradona's record, which had stood since 1976. He secured his position during the 2005–6 season, when he scored 18 goals in 36 matches. Atlético Madrid bought him in 2006, and he stayed there for five years. In his final season for Atlético, he was the third best goal scorer in Spain, behind Ronaldo and Messi. Agüero joined Manchester City in the 2011–12 season, and was the third best goal scorer in the Premier League behind Robin van Persie and Rooney. However, he made the year's most important and memorable goal when he scored against QPR in the final seconds of the last game of the season—claiming the Premier League title for Manchester City for the first time in 44 years.

Agüero was on Argentina's World Cup squad in 2010 but didn't get much play. Since then he has been growing as a player, and fans have high hopes for him and the Argentinean squad as a whole. He has obviously become one of the most powerful goal poachers in the world—fast and quick, shortish but strong as an ox, an incredibly industrious fighter. He was once married to Maradona's daughter, and they have a son together. What soccer genes that boy must have!

 Of Agüero's many qualities, perhaps the most important is his firepower whenever he sees an opening for a shot or pass.

 The words "fault" and "Agüero" hardly belong in the same sentence!

The sight of Balotelli in the uniform of the Italian squad strikes fear into the hearts of his opponents!

BALOTELLI
Striker
Italy
Born 1990
Plays for
AC Milan

BALOTELLI

"Why Always Me?"*

Balotelli was born in Palermo on June 12, 1990. His parents were poor immigrants from Ghana, and since they couldn't take care of him, he was fostered by an Italian couple. When Balotelli joined the Italian giants Inter Milan in 2007, two things were clear: that he would become a very powerful striker, and that his wild temper and personality would get him into all sorts of trouble. These two traits have followed him ever since. Manchester City bought Balotelli in 2010, and he scored 30 goals in 80 games before going back to Italy to play for AC Milan.

Balotelli played his first international game in 2010, two days before his 20th birthday. He was one of Italy's best players in Euro 2012 and is becoming more of a leader on the field. That's why the Italians call him Super Mario. Generally he scores in every other game.

* Balotelli revealed this message underneath his jersey after he scored a goal for Manchester City against Manchester United in October 2011. It seemed to be his way of saying that he gets too much attention. But he loves attention!

 Balotelli is quick and skillful, and has immense firepower. He is a strong and precise striker.

 Early in his career, Balotelli was so undisciplined that he was often sent off the field. Sometimes his poor judgment resulted in senseless tackles.

Brazil and Spain have argued over which country should enjoy Costa's talents. To look at this jersey, you might think he finally decided to play for Azerbaijan instead. But he's actually wearing the Atlético Madrid jersey, which has an ad on it from the Azerbaijan tourist authority.

COSTA
Striker
Spain
Born 1988
Plays for
Atlético Madrid

DIEGO COSTA
Passion and Diligence

Diego da Silva Costa was born in Lagarto, a small city in Brazil, on October 7, 1988. His family was poor, and there were no sports facilities in Lagarto, so he just played street ball with his friends. He thinks this early experience gave him his diligence and power, but for a long time he lacked discipline and order. He didn't start playing regulation soccer until he was 16, after his family had moved to the big city of São Paulo. Just two years later he joined a team from Portugal, and since 2007 he has played in Spain, mainly for

Atlético Madrid. Recently he's really come into his own: in the first 12 games of the 2013–14 season of La Liga, he scored 13 goals and seemed ready to beat Messi and Cristiano Ronaldo in points taken.

The Brazilians were displeased when Costa decided that he'd rather play internationally for Spain, since he'd become a Spanish citizen. Not many Brazilian kids would turn down the opportunity to wear that yellow jersey! In the Spanish squad's red jersey, Costa will be a lethal weapon in the 2014 World Cup.

Costa is as big and strong as an elephant, and seems to have endless endurance. His ability to score all kinds of goals is uncanny—he's always determined to find the back of the net!

Because his passion is so fierce, Costa is still prone to losing his temper.

DEMPSEY
Forward
U.S.A.
Born 1983
Plays for the
Seattle Sounders

Dempsey clashes with Steven Gerrard as the U.S. team ties England in the group stage of the 2010 World Cup.

+ Dempsey brings a ferocious energy to the field, and his ball-handling skills are impressive.

− When Dempsey is determined to hold onto the ball, he can get rough—and sometimes he's sent off the field.

CLINT DEMPSEY
Captain America

Clint Dempsey was born on March 9, 1983, in the small town of Nacogdoches, Texas. As a young boy, he was fascinated by the playing style of Diego Maradona and studied his moves on videotape. Dempsey started playing with elite youth teams in Dallas when he was 10, and eventually he became one of the top prospects in U.S. soccer. He made his professional debut with the New England Revolution in 2004, and in 2007 he moved to Fulham in the English Premier League. Dempsey was a standout in the Fulham side, twice being voted Player of the Season by the club's supporters. His 2012 transfer to Premier League powerhouse Tottenham made him the highest-paid U.S. soccer player of all time, but a year later he returned to his native soil to join the Seattle Sounders.

Dempsey played his first international game in 2004 and has since become a key part of the U.S. team. He's an aggressive attacker who can play any role in the offensive line, although he's most comfortable as a winger. In 2009, Dempsey was voted Man of the Match after he scored the winning goal in the United States' upset victory over Spain in the Confederations Cup semifinal, and in 2013 he was named captain of the U.S. team. Soccer fans in the U.S. are counting on Dempsey and his fellow attacker Landon Donovan to take the country to a strong finish in the 2014 World Cup.

Landon Donovan

Barcelona was always Fàbregas's favorite team, even though he went to Arsenal at an early age. When he finally put on the red and blue jersey, it was a dream come true.

FÀBREGAS
Attacking
midfielder
Spain
Born 1987
Plays for Barcelona

FÀBREGAS

Aggressive and Savvy

Cesc Fàbregas was born on May 4, 1987, in a town just outside Barcelona. He started playing for the local team when he was 10 years old. The coach wouldn't let him take the field against the Barcelona youth team, because he didn't want them to hear about this very promising young boy. But they found out anyway and got him into their youth academy. There he played with his contemporary and friend Lionel Messi. Fàbregas went to Arsenal in London when he was only 16 years old, because Arsène Wenger really believed in him. He played a lot at this very young age and did very well. Fàbregas mostly operates as an attacking midfielder, but he can play almost any attacking position if he needs to. He went home to Catalonia in 2011 and joined Messi and friends in Barcelona. Guardiola considered him a replacement for the magnificent Xavi in the midfield, but Fàbregas had trouble finding his role on the team at first. Recently he's been doing better and better, and his goals and assists are among the best.

Fàbregas was first selected for the Spanish national team in 2006, making him the youngest player to be picked in 70 years. Since then he's had a secure place on the squad and played in three big finals in a row: Euro 2008, World Cup 2010, and Euro 2012. Spain won them all!

 Just like Barcelona's other "tiki-taka" masters, Fàbregas has a great talent for interplay: he provides incredible assists and knows how to take action at critical moments.

 He is a bit unreliable and still has his bad games, probably because his managers keep changing his role on the field.

Falcao playing with Atlético Madrid against Espanyol in December 2011. He always wears gloves on the field.

FALCAO
Striker
Colombia
Born 1986
Plays for
AS Monaco

FALCAO
The Colombian Goal Machine

Radamel Falcao was born in Santa Marta, Colombia, on February 10, 1986. He was only 13 years and 199 days old when he played his first championship league game for Lanceros Boyacá in the Colombian second division, making him the youngest professional football player in the country's history. In 2001, he joined the giant Argentinean club River Plate. His aggressiveness was noticed, and in 2009 he went to Porto in Portugal, where he instantly became a star. In 2011, he was the top scorer in the Europa League, with 17 goals, and Porto won the league. In 2011, Falcao went to Atlético Madrid, where he became even more famous and won the Europa League again. In 2013, he went to Monaco. Falcao is considered one of the best strikers in the world, a regular goal machine: he scored 72 goals in 87 games with Porto, and 70 goals in 91 games with Atlético. He is equally good with either foot and also has a great header technique, even though he's not very tall.

Falcao started slowly with his national squad, but now he generally scores in every other game. He is the main reason the Colombians can hope for success in the World Cup in Brazil.

Falcao wearing the Monaco colors in the summer of 2013. The team is from the independent principality of Monaco in the south of France, but plays in the French league.

 Falcao is a natural goal scorer and very versatile. His talents as a playmaker are growing as well.

 Many people were surprised when Falcao went to Monaco, because the biggest clubs in Europe wanted him badly. The move made people think he might lack ambition, that he wants a fat paycheck rather than to play with the best.

GERRARD
General of the Midfield

Steven Gerrard was born in Liverpool, England, on May 30, 1980. He was recruited by Liverpool FC scouts at the age of nine and made his senior debut at 18 under the guidance of Gérard Houllier. A versatile player from an early age, Gerrard often filled in at right back and later played all across the midfield and even up front occasionally. He was a regular in the Liverpool midfield while still a teenager and soon tasted success as part of the squad that completed a treble in 2001, winning the UEFA Cup, the FA Cup, and the League Cup. His influence in the club kept growing: he became captain in 2003 and was instrumental in the unbelievable reversal in the 2005 Champions League final in Istanbul, where Liverpool came back from being down 3–0 at halftime against AC Milan. The next year brought the "Gerrard FA Cup final," in which Liverpool's inspirational captain dragged his team back from the brink of defeat to victory over West Ham.

Gerrard's energy in the midfield is unparalleled, but in recent years he's slowed down and taken on a more reserved role, preferring to dictate play from his half of the pitch rather than make lung-bursting runs into the opponent's penalty box. As Gerrard has matured, he has longed more and more for the honors that have escaped him so far: winning the English Premier League with Liverpool and a major tournament with England. With Liverpool resurgent, perhaps Gerrard can transfer some of his positive energy into success for his national side.

 Gerrard is a respected leader and possesses great vision and experience, which could prove crucial in England's quest for success.

 Gerrard will be 34 years old by the time the World Cup finals start. He doesn't have the stamina of his younger self, and his goal-scoring threat has diminished.

Gerrard is a living legend among Liverpool fans, having played for the Merseyside club his whole career, leading them to glory in the Champions League and the FA Cup.

GERRARD
Midfielder
England
Born 1980
Plays for
Liverpool

HAZARD

Hungry for Goals

Eden Hazard was born on January 7, 1991, in the Belgian city of La Louvière. He's one of several great Belgian players to have appeared in recent years. Hazard was 14 when he went to Lille in France, and he first played with the senior team in 2007, when he was 16. As he matured, he got a bigger role on the team, and during the 2010–11 season he scored 12 goals and provided 11 assists. Lille won the French league that season and also the Coupe de France. The next year Hazard scored 22 goals and provided 16 assists, and was voted Player of the Year in France, just two years after being named Young Player of the Year. Chelsea bought Hazard's contract in 2012, and in his first season in the English Premier League he scored 13 goals and provided 20 assists in all competitions. He has already been compared to players like Ronaldo and Messi, and he'll probably get even better as he matures.

Hazard played his first game for the Belgian national team in 2008. Some people think Belgium might even have what it takes to win the 2014 World Cup, especially with players like Hazard.

Eden Hazard playing with Chelsea. His younger brother Thorgan Hazard (born 1993) is also in the Chelsea camp and has already played one international game for Belgium.

HAZARD
Winger
Belgium
Born 1991
Plays for
Chelsea

Hazard is quick and inventive, and has great technique.

He is still young, and his lack of experience sometimes shows in big games.

INIESTA

The Quiet Magician

Andrés Iniesta was born on May 11, 1984, in a small village near Albacete, Spain. He joined Barcelona at the age of 12 and became part of the extremely powerful team they were putting together. Since 2002, Iniesta has been playing midfield for Barcelona with Xavi and other wizards. He is very quiet and inconspicuous, but his pinpoint passes can destroy the opponents' defense in an instant. He can also dribble magically through the defense.

Iniesta has played internationally for Spain since 2006 and has had a large part in the squad's unbelievable success, which began with their victory in Euro 2008, and then continued with their triumphs in the 2010 World Cup and Euro 2012. He will always be considered a god in Spain for scoring the winning goal in the final game of the 2010 World Cup in South Africa, when Spain took the trophy for the first time. And he'll play a key role in their attempt to retain the title in Brazil.

 Iniesta is famous for his passes and interplay, and it's almost impossible to take the ball away from him.

 Given his unbelievable skills, he should score more goals!

Xavi

INIESTA
Attacking
midfielder
Spain
Born 1984
Plays for Barcelona

Iniesta in the red and blue
uniform of Spain. Iniesta and his
teammate Xavi are masters at
keeping the ball until they find a
crack in the opponents' defense.

Lahm is half an inch taller than Lionel Messi. He is considered very short in Germany and is sometimes jokingly called the "Magic Dwarf," because of his fleet feet!

LAHM
Defensive
midfielder
Germany
Born 1983
Plays for
Bayern Munich

LAHM
The Little Leader

Philipp Lahm was born in Munich on November 11, 1983. He started playing soccer with his local team but was invited to join Bayern Munich at age 11. From the beginning, he played in the defense. He joined the second team when he was 17 years old, and started playing for the first team in 2002, when he had just turned 19. Then he was sent on loan to Stuttgart so he could gain first-team experience in the Bundesliga. Lahm played 71 games for Stuttgart before returning home for the 2005–6 season. Since then he's been a key player for Bayern, and has won everything it's possible to win for them. Lahm has long been recognized as one of the best right fullbacks in the world, although he is able to play every defensive role. An immensely versatile player, he's good at attacking, too. Guardiola has often placed him in the midfield with good results. Wherever Lahm is positioned, he's always an effective leader—he's been Bayern's captain since 2011.

Lahm played his first game for the German national team in 2004, when he was 20 years old, and was on the German squad in Euro 2004. Since then he's taken part in big tournament finals every other summer and has only gotten better. He's been the captain of the German national team since 2010, and he just might lift the winning trophy in Brazil this summer.

 Guardiola, the new Bayern manager, says Lahm is the most intelligent soccer player he's worked with. That's a big compliment from someone who's coached Messi, Xavi, Iniesta, and other masters of the game.

 Lahm is only 5 feet 7 inches tall, which is sometimes a drawback when he's dealing with tall strikers.

LUKAKU
The Mountain

Romelu Lukaku was born in Antwerp, Belgium, on May 13, 1993. It soon became clear that he was a magnificent striker with a real nose for the goal. He scored 121 goals in 68 games for the Lierse youth team! He joined Belgium's strongest club, Anderlecht, when he was 16 and started playing in the first division right away. Even though he was young and often a substitute, he scored in almost every other game. He went to Chelsea at 18 but didn't get many opportunities and was loaned to WBA and then to Everton. He is very popular at Everton due to his enthusiasm and aggressiveness—plus he keeps scoring goals.

Lukaku was only 17 when he played his first international game and scored his first goals for Belgium. Like Eden Hazard, he is part of a young and very promising Belgian national team that will be exciting to watch in the World Cup in Brazil. Some people think they might even make it all the way! Lukaku's Everton teammate Kevin Mirallas is also on the Belgian team, along with Marouane Fellaini (Manchester United), Christian Benteke (Aston Villa), Jan Vertonghen, Moussa Dembélé, and Nacer Chadli (all Tottenham players), Kevin De Bruyne (Chelsea), Vincent Kompany (Manchester City), Thomas Vermaelen (Arsenal), and goalkeepers Thibaut Courtois (Atlético Madrid) and Simon Mignolet (Liverpool). This team should go far with Lukaku on the firing line!

 Lukaku is tall and strong, and always looking for goal opportunities.

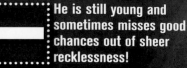 He is still young and sometimes misses good chances out of sheer recklessness!

Lukaku is from a family of great soccer players. His father was an international player for the People's Republic of the Congo (or Zaire, as it was then called). But Lukaku was born in Belgium.

LUKAKU
Striker
Belgium
Born 1993
Plays for
Everton

MESSI

The Best

Lionel Messi was born in Rosario, Argentina, on June 24, 1987. As a boy, he suffered from a growth hormone deficiency. He wouldn't have reached even 4 feet 11 inches without hormone injections, which his family couldn't afford. But Messi had already shown considerable soccer talent despite his height, and Barcelona asked him to join their club. Barça paid for his shots, and when Messi got taller, his talent became even more obvious. Of course, it can be hard to say for sure whether one soccer player is better than another, but most people agree that Messi is not just the best player of our time, but one of the best in history—and he's far from finished.

With Barcelona, Messi has won every available title and beaten most goal-scoring records. During the 2011–12 season, he scored 73 goals in 60 games for Barcelona! The only title left for Messi to win is the World Cup with Argentina, and that is his greatest dream. If he manages to achieve it, he will finally prove to Argentina and the whole world that he's the equal of Diego Maradona. Maradona, incidentally, was the manager of the great Argentinean national team when Messi and his teammates lost in the quarterfinals of the 2010 World Cup. They don't want to see a repeat of that!

 Messi is a uniquely skilled dribbler and a terrific shooter, with a keen eye for interplay and unexpected possibilities.

 He can do everything! He has no faults in his game.

Messi with his eyes on the ball. No one can match his technique— and probably no one ever has.

Barcelona teammates Messi and Neymar will be opponents in the 2014 World Cup.

MESSI
Striker
Argentina
Born 1987
Plays for
Barcelona

Modrić in action in the white Real Madrid jersey.

MODRIĆ
Midfielder
Croatia
Born 1985
Plays for
Real Madrid

MODRIĆ
The Croatian Cruyff

Luka Modrić was born in Zadar, Croatia, on September 9, 1985. He joined the best team in Croatia, Dinamo Zagreb, when he was 16, and immediately stood out as a promising midfielder. When he was 18, he went on loan to a team in neighboring Bosnia and Herzegovina and did so well that he was voted the best player in the league. This achievement is particularly impressive because Modrić is short and thin, and the Bosnian league has always been considered rough—but he has often surprised people with his power and guts. Modrić was a Croatian champion with Dinamo Zagreb three years in a row, but in 2008 he went to Tottenham. There

he became a fan favorite for his cool and classy playing style. He's usually a play-maker, but can take on different roles in midfield. He often attacks and also stays in front of his own defense. His skills have earned him the nickname "the Croatian Cruyff"—a reference to the Dutch master Johan Cruyff. Modrić's the kind of player who can win a game with one accurate assist through the opponents' defense. In 2012, he went to Real Madrid.

Modrić has been a key player on the Croatian national team since 2006. He will undoubtedly make an impact in the World Cup finals in Brazil.

 Modrić's superior technique and many skills make him one of the best midfielders in the world.

 Given his talents, some people think he should score more goals. And he can be stopped if he is closely guarded.

Müller playing for Bayern Munich. By the end of March 2014, Müller had scored 95 goals in 244 games for Bayern. He had also scored 16 goals in 47 international games.

MÜLLER
Striker
Germany
Born 1989
Plays for
Bayern Munich

MÜLLER
A Versatile Attacker

Thomas Müller was born in Weilheim, Germany, on September 13, 1989, and started playing soccer with TSV Pähl. His talent soon became apparent, and at age 10 he joined Bayern Munich's youth academy. Müller played a few games with the first team in the 2008–9 season and secured his place on the squad in the next season. After a brilliant start and lots of goals, all eyes were on Müller, but he withstood the pressure and played like a mature veteran. Bayern Munich won both the Bundesliga and the DFB Cup, and Müller played in every game of the season. He scored 13 goals in the league, making him Bayern's second best goal scorer. He also provided 11 assists. In the DFB Cup, he scored four goals and provided two assists. Over the last few years, Müller has continued to be an integral part of Bayern's fabulous team. In the great 2012–13 season, Müller scored 23 goals in 43 games.

With only two international games under his belt, Müller might have seemed like a surprising pick for the German squad in the 2010 World Cup. But he turned out to be the tournament's top scorer, with five goals and three assists! He was also voted the Best Young Player of the Tournament. In 2013, he played eight international games for Germany and scored six goals. Müller is still young and has the potential to go even farther.

 Müller is a big, strong, and versatile forward who can play as a striker, attacking midfielder, or winger. Power and daring are his traits.

 It's hardly his fault, but his versatility often poses a problem. His managers have trouble finding the right role for him.

Neuer playing for Germany against Austria in September 2012. The three stars above his badge stand for Germany's three World Cup wins, in 1954, 1974, and 1990. The Germans are ready to add that fourth star!

NEUER
Goalkeeper
Germany
Born 1986
Plays with
Bayern Munich

NEUER

Shut and Locked

Manuel Neuer was born in Gelsenkirchen, Germany, on March 27, 1986. He was five years old when he started training with Schalke, and he also attended Gesamtschule Berger Feld, a school that emphasizes sports. Many boys who later became soccer pros also went there, including Mesut Özil. Neuer played for Schalke until 2011, when Bayern Munich bought him, which was not surprising: by then he was the best goalkeeper in Germany, and he was voted Player of the Year in the Bundesliga. He was not only reliable in the goal but also had a good influence on his defenders. Neuer and his teammates will probably always remember the 2012–13 season, when Bayern won three titles: the Bundesliga, the DFB Cup, and the UEFA Champions League. Neuer was a big part of that success: for instance, he kept a clean sheet four games in a row against Juventus and Barcelona.

Neuer played his first international game in 2009 and was Germany's main goalkeeper in the 2010 World Cup. He was selected for the Euro 2012 Team of the Tournament.

 Neuer has great reflexes, and it's almost impossible to get the ball past him. He's also good at getting the ball back in play.

 A goalkeeper with his kind of record has no outstanding faults. Of course, he can have a bad day—but nobody remembers the last time that happened!

NEYMAR

The New Pelé

Neymar da Silva Santos Júnior was born on February 5, 1992, in a suburb of São Paulo, one of the biggest cities in the world. His tremendous soccer skills were apparent early on, and he started playing for the Santos' first team in 2009. In his first season, he scored 14 goals in 48 games in all competitions and provided 19 assists. The next year he did even better, with 42 goals in 60 games and 19 assists. And that was just the beginning. Brazilians compare him to the great Pelé. Both are equally good as strikers and as playmakers, and Neymar often takes a turn as a winger, too. His ball technique is amazing; his speed, massive; his power, unbelievable; and his courage, absolute. Europe heard about Neymar's skills, and many clubs tried to sign him before he finally went to Barcelona in 2013. With Barça, his performance has only continued to improve.

Neymar played his first international game in 2010, but he wasn't on the Brazilian squad in that year's World Cup. He was, however, on the Brazilian squad that won the Confederations Cup in 2013, and then he showed what he was all about. He scored four goals and was voted the Best Player of the Tournament! There have already been claims, especially in Brazil, that Neymar is the best soccer player in the world. Now he has a chance to prove it on home soil, in the 2014 World Cup.

 On a good day, it seems like Neymar can do anything he wants with the ball.

 Occasionally, when he was younger, he performed some elegant dives.

The Brazilians have high hopes for Neymar. He's supposed to lead them to victory in the World Cup on home soil.

NEYMAR
Forward
Brazil
Born 1992
Plays for
Barcelona

Teammates at Barcelona, opponents in the World Cup: Neymar and Messi.

Oscar playing for Brazil against Uruguay.

OSCAR
Playmaker
Brazil
Born 1991
Plays for
Chelsea

OSCAR

A New Genius

Oscar was born on September 9, 1991, in a suburb of the huge metropolis of São Paulo. He started out playing for his local team, but scouts from São Paulo FC recruited him when he was 13. Oscar stayed with São Paulo for six years, winning the Brazilian league with them in 2008. After a contract dispute in 2009, he switched to another Brazilian club, Internacional, where he remained for two seasons, playing 35 games and scoring 11 goals. To fulfill his ambition of becoming a better soccer player, he accepted an offer from Chelsea in 2012. He has done very well there. Oscar's style is aggressive yet classy. He usually plays as an attacking midfielder, and sometimes as a winger.

Oscar was first selected for the Brazilian national team in 2011. He was on the Brazilian squad that took the silver in the 2012 Olympics in London, and the one that captured the 2013 Confederations Cup. Brazil is known for producing midfielders who are true artists when it comes to passing, interplay, and vision. After Oscar and Paulinho's strong performance in the Confederations Cup, the Brazilians expect them to take the place of past geniuses like Zico, Kaká, and Ronaldinho.

 Oscar keeps the ball easily, and his dribbles through the defense can be awesome.

 He is still young, and his performances can still be inconsistent.

Özil got off to a great start with Arsenal, and the fans idolized him almost immediately. Here he's playing against Southampton in late November 2013.

ÖZIL
Playmaker
Germany
Born 1988
Plays for Arsenal

ÖZIL

The Master of the Assist

Mesut Özil was born in Gelsenkirchen, Germany, on October 15, 1988. He is of Turkish descent, but he always wanted to play for the country of his birth. Özil began his career with Schalke but moved at an early age to Werder Bremen, where he began to attract attention as a promising young midfielder. After his performance with the lively German national team in the 2010 World Cup, Real Madrid signed him. He flourished there as an attacking midfielder and a playmaker, scoring magnificent goals and making great passes. It came as a surprise when he was sold to Arsenal in the fall of 2013, but in his very very first games with the English club he showed that he was one of the best players in his position.

Özil is very skilled and resourceful, and sees chances that most players overlook. He has been called "the New Messi" or "the New Zidane," but his manager at Real Madrid, José Mourinho, put it differently, saying, "Özil is unique. There is no copy of him—not even a bad copy." On Germany's magnificent national team, Özil is the driving force.

 Özil can win games on his own. In the 2012–13 season, he scored 10 goals for Real Madrid, but provided 26 assists!

 He is slightly built, and sometimes it seems like he doesn't have the stamina to play a full 90 minutes. His strength can fade out in the later stages of a game.

RIBÉRY
The Wild Beast

Franck Ribéry was born on April 7, 1983, in Boulogne-sur-Mer in the north of France. He was in a car accident when he was two years old, which is how he got the scars on his face. Unlike many other first-rate players, he did not attract attention as a youngster, and at the beginning of his career he moved around from club to club. It was not until he joined Marseille in 2005 that people started to notice him. Playing as a left winger, he managed to harness his power and keep moving forward on the field. His performance at Marseille resulted in an offer from Bayern Munich, where he has flourished ever since, winning every available title. Defenders on opposing teams

Ribéry, focused as always, playing for the French national team.

dread the sight of Ribéry coming at them like a wild beast.

Ribéry was on the French national squad that came in second in the 2006 World Cup in Germany, and also on the one that did very poorly in the 2010 World Cup in South Africa. How France will do in 2014 depends very much on Ribéry.

RIBÉRY
Forward
France
Born 1983
Plays for
Bayern Munich

+ Ribéry is extremely tricky, keeps the ball well, shoots accurately, and has an eye for passes. He is very imaginative, and you never know his next move.

− He has been prone to injury over the years.

ROBBEN
Winger
The Netherlands
Born 1984
Plays for
Bayern Munich

Robben in the famous orange
uniform of the Dutch national team.

ARJEN ROBBEN

A Lethal Left Foot

Arjen Robben was born on January 23, 1984, in a small village close to the Dutch city of Groningen. His ball-handling skills have been incredible ever since he was a boy, thanks to his tireless practice. He started his career at Groningen, became a star with PSV Eindhoven, and joined Chelsea when he was 20. He's a left footer, but has usually played on the right wing—although he can take the field in any attacking position. In 2007, he went to Real Madrid and did well there, but he was sold to Bayern Munich two years later to make room for Cristiano Ronaldo and Kaká. Robben was not too happy about that, but he recovered quickly and is getting better and better with Bayern. He scores more goals than ever before, and his partnership with Franck Ribéry on the other wing is a big part of the squad's success.

Robben played in his first international game in 2003. Few people possess his skills and aggressiveness, and he has an important role in the free and easy play of the Dutch squad.

 When Robben approaches the edge of the penalty area from the right wing and moves the ball to his left leg, the whole world knows his plan. Still, the ball seems to end up in the top far corner of the goal remarkably often.

 He can be very selfish, because he loves the ball! This has made him controversial, as both a player and a person.

CRISTIANO RONALDO
Always Getting Better

Cristiano Ronaldo dos Santos Aveiro was born on the Portuguese island of Madeira on February 5, 1985. He grew up poor and supposedly never had any toys. His career can be described very briefly: his unique abilities, together with his focus and ambition, have made him one of the best soccer players in history. Interestingly, even though Ronaldo has been overshadowed by Messi for the past couple years, this has not discouraged him at all, but only spurred him on to greater achievements.

Ronaldo is still getting better, and he'll give all he has in the 2014 World Cup. Portugal may not have a strong enough team to get to the top, but Ronaldo will take them as far as they can go, that's for sure.

 Ronaldo can simply do everything. He is a die-hard driving force.

— A strong defense used to be able to press him so hard that he sort of . . . disappeared. Probably not any more, though.

When Ronaldo was younger, his performances in big games often lacked grit. But that has changed: now he loves those crucial moments the most. In November 2013, he secured Portugal's place in the World Cup by scoring a hat trick in this away game against Sweden.

RONALDO
Forward
Portugal
Born 1985
Plays for
Real Madrid

49

ROONEY

The Bulldog

ROONEY
Forward
England
Born 1985
Plays for
Manchester United

Rooney scoring his famous goal for Manchester United against rival Manchester City on February 12, 2011. Rooney can do a lot!

Wayne Rooney was born on October 24, 1985, in Croxteth, a suburb of Liverpool. He started out playing with his local team and joined Everton when he was nine years old. His hunger for goals was out of this world: the year he turned 11, he scored 114 goals in 29 games. He played two seasons for the Everton senior team, and then Manchester United bought him in 2004 for 25.6 million pounds—a record-breaking amount for a teenage player.

Rooney played in his first international game in 2003, making him the youngest to go out for England up to that time. He is likely to become the top goal scorer of all time not only for England but also for Manchester United. With ManU, Rooney has won the English Premier League five times, the FA Cup three times, and the 2008 UEFA Champions League. He has also received all kinds of individual accolades in his career, and is generally considered the best English player of recent years. Some players are said to be able to win games on their own, and on a good day, Rooney is one of them. He is always threatening, and beyond his soccer skills, he possesses unusual power and a keen will to win.

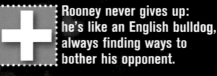

Rooney never gives up: he's like an English bulldog, always finding ways to bother his opponent.

Sometimes he tries too hard. And while he certainly has great skills, ball-handling is not his strongest asset.

SÁNCHEZ
Fast and Flexible!

Alexis Sánchez was born on December 19, 1988, in the town of Tocopilla, Chile. He first played for Cobreloa in his home country, but in 2006 he was sold to Udinese in Italy. They loaned him out right away, first to Colo-Colo in Chile and then to River Plate in Argentina. That's how Udinese—and many other clubs—handle promising players who need to gain experience. The young Sánchez did well, winning the league with both teams. Next he played three seasons for Udinese, scoring 12 goals in the last one. In 2011, he joined Barcelona, with whom he won the Copa del Rey in 2012 and La Liga in 2013. It took Sánchez a long time to settle into the Barcelona squad, and for a while he seemed shy around all the geniuses, but now he's really coming into his own.

Sánchez played his first game for Chile in 2006, and his role on the national squad has gotten bigger over the years.

 Sánchez can play every attacking position and usually takes the field as a forward or a winger. He's incredibly fast and very skillful with the ball.

 A lack of confidence can neutralize his energy completely.

SÁNCHEZ
Forward
Chile
Born 1988
Plays for
Barcelona

Sánchez always does his best on the field. If he hits a hot streak, Chile might threaten the big countries in the 2014 World Cup.

SILVA
Central
defender
Brazil
Born 1984
Plays for Paris
Saint-Germain

The last time the World Cup was held in Brazil was in 1950, and Brazil lost the final game to Uruguay. The country was devastated. Thiago Silva and his teammates know they can't let that happen again in 2014.

THIAGO SILVA
The Elegant Defender

Thiago Silva was born in the Brazilian metropolis of Rio de Janeiro on September 22, 1984. He played with Fluminense in his home city until he was 16, and then he started globe-trotting, staying in the camps of Porto and Dynamo Moscow, among others. By that time, he'd settled into the role of central defender, after earlier stints as a winger or defensive midfielder. In 2006, he returned to Fluminense and played with them for two seasons. He joined AC Milan in 2009 and won the Italian division with them in the 2011–12 season. He was voted Defender of the Year and also selected for the Team of the Year, and in the next season he was AC Milan's captain. Paris Saint-Germain (PSG) signed Silva in the summer of 2012, and in his first season the team won the French league. Barcelona tried to lure him away the following summer, but he decided to stay in Paris.

Silva was not a child prodigy. He was 24 when he played his first international game in 2008. He was on the Brazilian squad that won the bronze in the 2008 Olympics and then the silver in the 2012 Olympics, after he'd become the team captain. Silva led his team to victory in the Confederations Cup in 2013 and may very well lift the World Cup trophy on home soil in July. He's one of the most reliable central defenders in the world. He uses his formidable understanding of the game to defend, so he doesn't have to get rough. Because of that, he rarely gets booked.

+ It goes without saying that you don't get to be Brazil's captain unless you're a pretty decent player.

− Some people think Silva's not decisive enough on the field.

Sturridge in the Liverpool uniform, threatening the Swansea goal in February 2013. He played 16 games for Liverpool in the 2012–13 season, scoring 11 goals.

STURRIDGE
Striker
England
Born 1989
Plays for
Liverpool

STURRIDGE
Quick and Cunning

Daniel Sturridge was born in Birmingham on September 1, 1989. He started training with Aston Villa when he was seven and joined Manchester City when he was 14. That was when Manchester City was still just a middling English club, before it was taken over by Sheikh Mansour of Abu Dhabi. Sturridge got his first chance with the senior team in 2007 and stood out as a very promising striker. Chelsea signed him in 2009, but he didn't manage to secure his place, so he was loaned to Bolton for half a season, where he did very well. In January 2013, Chelsea sold him to Liverpool, where he has flourished, to put it mildly. After playing as a winger at Chelsea, he's a striker again, and his partnership with Luis Suárez is magnificent.

Sturridge played for all of England's junior national teams, and his first game for the senior team was in 2011. He didn't play much with the national team to begin with, but his recent performances with Liverpool make it certain he'll be a key player in the World Cup.

 Sturridge is fast as lightning and possesses great technique.

 His confidence matters a lot—without it, his performance crashes. But that's true of other players, too.

Suárez in the Liverpool uniform. He was one of the main reasons Uruguay did so well in the 2010 World Cup.

SUÁREZ
Forward
Uruguay
Born 1987
Plays for
Liverpool

SUÁREZ
The Fiery Forward

Luis Suárez was born in Salto, Uruguay, on January 24, 1987. Uruguay is a soccer-crazy country, and its success has been incredible, considering it has a population of only 3.3 million. Suárez started his career with Nacional in Montevideo, the country's capital. Right away he attracted attention for his skills and his hunger for goals, but also for his temper, which has always been hard for him to control. He went to Groningen in the Netherlands when he was 19, and then he became a star playing for Ajax in Amsterdam. He scored a lot of goals for Ajax and seemed to be well on his way to managing his temper. He joined Liverpool in 2011, and the fans there love his die-hard fighting spirit and all the tricks and stunts in his style. When Suárez has a good day, he can perform like nobody else. As a result, he scores in more than half his games. He also helps his teammates a lot, both with his incredible passes and by attracting the defense's attention.

Suárez is as passionate about the Uruguayan national team as he is about his clubs. He helped take Uruguay to a fourth-place finish in the 2010 World Cup, scoring some great goals before he was suspended for deliberately blocking a shot with his hand in the quarterfinals against Ghana.

Suárez has every trait a good forward should, but he's probably at his best dribbling through a thick defensive wall with the ball glued to his feet.

He's often been accused of diving and dishonesty, and he's been suspended for racial abuse and twice for biting an opponent.

YAYA TOURÉ
The Train

Gnégnéri Yaya Touré was born on May 13, 1983, in Bouaké, the second largest city in the Ivory Coast. In 2001, he went to play in Europe. He was no child prodigy, but his hard work in the midfield paid off at last, and he joined Barcelona in 2007. Touré attracted attention in Barcelona for his power and work ethic, but Pep Guardiola, the club's new manager, could not guarantee him a place on the first team. So Touré joined Manchester City, where he's truly come into his own. He's an active midfielder, a bulldozer in the defensive line. Sometimes he charges forward like a train and scores a beautiful goal. You might say he's the heart of Manchester City's powerful squad.

Touré was voted African Footballer of the Year in 2011 and 2012. The Ivory Coast's national team has many strong players, including their captain Didier Drogba, Salomon Kalou, Gervinho, and Yaya's big brother Kolo Touré. This squad could do well in the World Cup, and the energetic Touré will probably figure prominently.

 Touré is big and imposing—and impossible to stop when he's going full steam ahead.

 Even though he's surprisingly agile for his size, dexterity is not his strongest point.

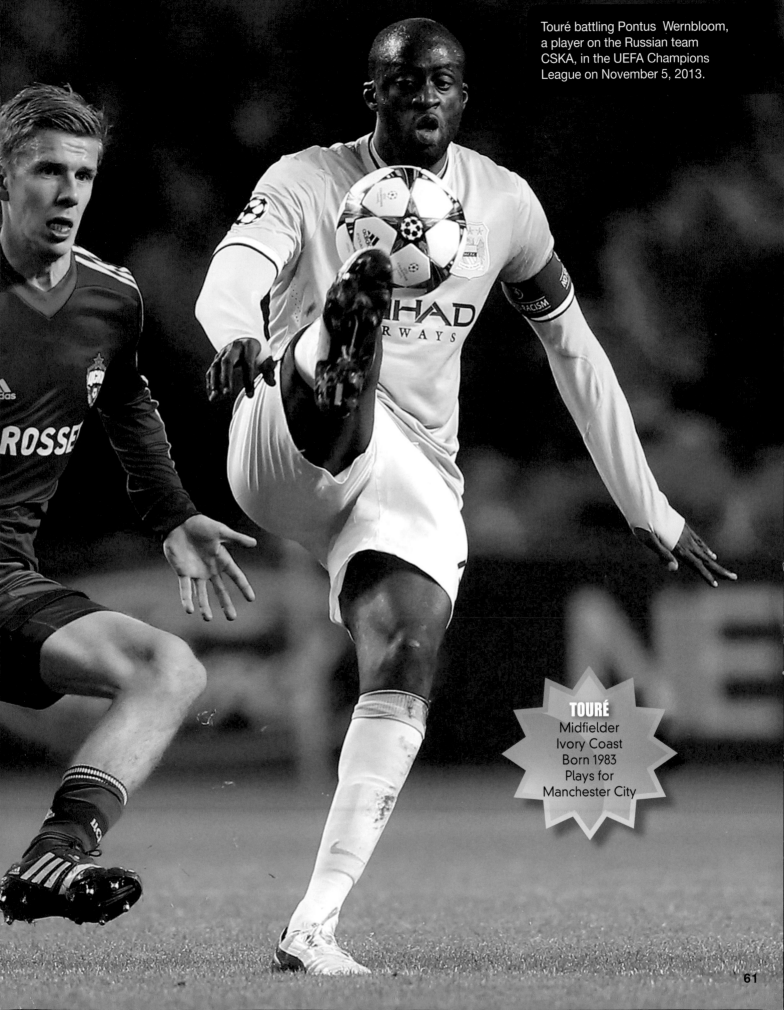

Touré battling Pontus Wernbloom, a player on the Russian team CSKA, in the UEFA Champions League on November 5, 2013.

TOURÉ
Midfielder
Ivory Coast
Born 1983
Plays for
Manchester City

ROBIN VAN PERSIE

The Artist

Robin van Persie was born in the Dutch port city of Rotterdam on August 6, 1983. His parents are both artists, but he says his own creative outlet is soccer. Some of his goals and assists truly are works of art! He started playing for Feyenoord in his home city, but in 2004 Arsène Wenger got him to join Arsenal. At first he played as a left winger, but then he became a versatile striker. He scores goals of all kinds, takes free kicks and corner kicks, and has a keen eye for passes and interplay. After eight years with Arsenal he joined Manchester United and secured the league title for the team almost singehandedly in the 2012–13 season.

Van Persie played his first international game for the Netherlands in 2005 and has scored in the finals of the last four big competitions. The Dutch ended the 2010 World Cup in second place, and they hope to take the trophy in Brazil! Van Persie will give it everything he's got, and he's only improved in recent years.

 Van Persie is very versatile and scores goals of all shapes and sizes. He's always working to further his team's cause.

 He was ill-tempered and injury prone early on, but he's managed to rid himself of these faults.